I0464104

The Cryptocurrency Called Bitcoin

Lee Maxwell

© 2017

© Copyright 2017 by Lee Maxwell - All rights reserved.

This document is geared towards providing exact and reliable information in regards to the topic and issue covered. The publication is sold with the idea that the publisher is not required to render accounting, officially permitted, or otherwise, qualified services. If advice is necessary, legal or professional, a practiced individual in the profession should be ordered.

- From a Declaration of Principles which was accepted and approved equally by a Committee of the American Bar Association and a Committee of Publishers and Associations.

In no way is it legal to reproduce, duplicate, or transmit any part of this document in either electronic means or in printed format. Recording of this publication is strictly prohibited and any storage of this document is not allowed unless with written permission from the publisher. All rights reserved.

The information provided herein is stated to be truthful and consistent, in that any liability, in terms of inattention or otherwise, by any usage or abuse of any policies, processes, or directions contained within is the solitary and utter responsibility of the recipient reader. Under no circumstances will any legal responsibility or blame be held against the publisher for any reparation, damages, or monetary loss due to the information herein, either directly or indirectly.

Respective authors own all copyrights not held by the publisher.

The information herein is offered for informational purposes solely, and is universal as so. The presentation of the information is without contract or any type of guarantee assurance.

The trademarks that are used are without any consent, and the publication of the trademark is without permission or backing by the trademark owner. All trademarks and brands within this book are for clarifying purposes only and are the owned by the owners themselves, not affiliated with this document.

Disclaimer and Terms of Use: The Author and Publisher has strived to be as accurate and complete as possible in the creation of this book, notwithstanding the fact that he does not warrant or represent at any time that the contents within are accurate due to the rapidly changing nature of the Internet. While all attempts have been made to verify information provided in this publication, the Author and Publisher assumes no responsibility for errors, omissions, or contrary interpretation of the subject matter herein. Any perceived slights of specific persons, peoples, or organizations are unintentional. In practical advice books, like anything else in life, there are no guarantees of results. Readers are cautioned to rely on their own judgment about their individual circumstances and act accordingly. This book is not intended for use as a source of legal, medical, business, accounting or financial advice. All readers are advised to seek services of competent professionals in the legal, medical, business, accounting, and finance fields.

TABLE OF CONTENTS

INTRODUCTION TO CRYPTOCURRENCY

Cryptocurrency is a decentralized payment system, which basically lets people send currency to each other over the web without the need for a trusted third party such as a bank or financial institution. The transactions are cheap, and in many cases, they're free. And also, the payments are pseudo anonymous as well. The main feature is that it's totally decentralized, which means that there's no single central point of authority or anything like that.

The high level of anonymity in there means that it's very hard to trace transactions. It's not totally impossible, but it's impractical in most cases. So crime with cryptocurrency-- because you've got fast, borderless transactions, and you've got a high level of anonymity, it in theory creates a system that is ripe for exploitation. So in most cases when it's a crime online with online payment systems, then they tend to go to the authorities and, say, we can hand over this payment information or we can stop these transactions and reverse them.

Cryptocurrency is electronic currency, short and simple. However, what's not so short and simple is exactly how it comes to have value. It is a digitized, virtual, decentralized currency produced by the application of cryptography, which, according to Merriam Webster dictionary, is the "computerized encoding and decoding of information". Cryptography is the foundation that makes debit cards, computer banking and eCommerce systems possible.

The way cryptocurrency is brought into existence is quite fascinating. Unlike gold, which has to be mined from the ground, cryptocurrency is merely an entry in a virtual ledger which is stored in various computers around the world. These entries have to be 'mined' using mathematical algorithms. Individual users or, more likely, a group of users run computational analysis to find particular series of data, called blocks. The 'miners' find data that produces an exact pattern to the cryptographic algorithm. At that point, it's applied to the series, and they've found a block. After an equivalent data series on the block matches up with the algorithm, the block of data has been unencrypted. The miner gets a reward of a specific amount of cryptocurrency. As time goes on, the amount of the reward decreases as the cryptocurrency becomes scarcer. Adding to that, the complexity of the algorithms in the search for new blocks is also increased. Computationally, it becomes harder to find a matching series. Both of these scenarios come together to decrease the speed in which cryptocurrency is created. This imitates the difficulty and scarcity of mining a commodity like gold.

Now, anyone can be a miner. The originators of Bitcoin made the mining tool open source, so it's free to anyone. However, the computers they use run 24 hours a day, seven days a week. The algorithms are extremely complex and the CPU is running full tilt. Many users have specialized computers made specifically for mining cryptocurrency. Both the user and the specialized computer are called miners.

Miners (the human ones) also keep ledgers of transactions and act as auditors, so that a coin isn't duplicated in any way. This keeps the system from being hacked and from running amok. They're paid for this work by receiving new cryptocurrency every week that they maintain their operation. They keep their cryptocurrency in specialized files on their computers or other personal devices. These files are called wallets.

HOW CRYPTOCURRENCY PROFIT YOUR BUSINESS

Cryptocurrency is a means to purchase, sell, and invest that completely avoids both government oversight and banking systems tracking the movement of your money. In a world economy that is destabilized, this system can become a stable force. Also gives you a great deal of anonymity. Unfortunately this can lead to misuse by a criminal element using cryptocurrency to their own ends just as regular money can be misused. However, it can also keep the government from tracking your every purchase and invading your personal privacy.

When most people think of cryptocurrency they might as well be thinking of cryptic currency. Very few people seem to know what it is and for some reason everyone seems to be talking about it as if they do. This book will hopefully demystify all the aspects of cryptocurrency and bitcoin so that by the time you're finished reading you will have a pretty good idea of what it is and what it's all about.

You may find that cryptocurrency is for you or you may not but at least you'll be able to speak with a degree of certainty and knowledge that others won't possess.There are many people who have already reached millionaire status by dealing in the cryptocurrency called bitcoin. Clearly there's a lot of money in this brand new industry.

Cryptocurrency isn't backed by banks; it's not backed by a government, but by an extremely complicated arrangement of algorithms. Cryptocurrency is electricity which is encoded into complex strings of algorithms. What lend monetary value are their intricacy and their security from hackers. The way that crypto currency is made is simply too difficult to reproduce.

Cryptocurrency is in direct opposition to what is called fiat money. Fiat money is currency that gets its worth from government ruling or law. The dollar, the yen, and the Euro are all examples. Any currency that is defined as legal tender is fiat money.

Unlike fiat money, another part of what makes crypto currency valuable is that, like a commodity such as silver and gold, there's only a finite amount of it. Only 21,000,000 of these extremely complex algorithms were produced. No more, no less. It can't be altered by printing more of it, like a government printing more money to pump up the system without backing. Or by a bank altering a digital ledger, something the Federal Reserve will instruct banks to do to adjust for inflation.

Cryptocurrency comes in quite a few forms. Bitcoin was the first and is the standard from which all other cryptocurrencies pattern themselves. All are produced by meticulous alpha-numerical computations from a complex coding tool. Some other cryptocurrencies are Litecoin, Namecoin, Peercoin, Dogecoin, and Worldcoin, to name a few. These are called altcoins as a generalized name. The prices of each are regulated by the supply of the specific cryptocurrency and the demand that the market has for that currency.

LIST OF CRYPTOCURRENCIES

Although there are technically over 1000 cryptocurrencies, only handfuls are relevant. Of those, even less have a market cap above $1 million. Below is a list of cryptocurrencies and additional resources you can use to learn more about the different cryptocurrency types.

List of Top Cryptocurrencies

• **Bitcoin**: Bitcoin is an easy pick. It was the first cryptocurrency, it has the highest market cap, it's coins are worth the most (about $225 USD as of June 2015), it's the most familiar and invested-in coin, it's a lot of things... primarily Bitcoin is the reason anyone is talking about cryptocurrency in the first place. You might not want to start a CPU-based Bitcoin mining company in 2015 or start buying coins for $225 a pop... but it's still going to take 1st place on our list.

• **Litecoin**: Litecoin is probably the second most important digital coin. It has the third-highest market cap as of June 2015, CPU mining is still sort of possible, people know what a Litecoin is, it uses essentially the same technology of Bitcoin, and it is worth about 1/100th of what a Bitcoin is on a good day. Really, a Litecoin is a lot like a

Bitcoin before the whole 'Silk Road' controversy, or as some people would say "a Litecoin is like a Bitcoin except with the value a reasonable person would expect a digital coin to have in a rational market… ie between $1 – $10 USD.".

• **Dogecoin**: Dogecoin (like the "Doge" internet meme about a dog and misspelling) has the 7th highest Market cap as of June 2015, individual coins aren't worth as much as other coins on the list (about $0.001 on the dollar on a good day as of June 2015) but its value and popularity have remained steady. Dogecoin essentially uses the same technology as Bitcoin (with a few important technical distinctions to be fair). Like the failed Coinye West, Dogecoin was just in it for the lolz (ie it was created as a joke), but unlike Coinye, Dogecoin became inexplicably popular. Why do we suggest a joke coin? Because it's a popular coin and today the only funny part about it is the name (and it's mascot / backstory). Really, it's a lot like Litecoin — a fairly priced coin with some consumer confidence as of 2015. Dogecoin has turnedtheir comedic origins into an excuse to make their coin "fun and friendly", which was a smart long-term move. It's also one of the only major cryptocurrencies with a .com Top-Level Domain name and is one of the few that attempts to reach an audience outside of techies and cryptography nerds.

• **Namecoin**: Ok really, really, Namecoin is almost exactly the same as Bitcoin. It was the first "fork" of the Bitcoin software (ie. it's based on Bitcoin and has the same unit cap, but has a few tweaks as to how data is stored). Namecoin was originally just going to be an upgrade to Bitcoin, but people were nervous that it would pose issues. So Namecoin is basically Bitcoin, but like everything not-Namecoin is worth just a fraction of Bitcoin. Its solid background and reasonable price point (about $0.40 on the dollar as of June 2015) makes it a relatively good coin to invest in.

• **Darkcoin (Dash):** Darkcoin, known as Dash as of March 25, 2015 (dash=digital cash) but previously known as XCoin, is the most unique (functionality-wise) of the coins we have discussed so far. XCoin was developed by Evan Duffield who wanted to improve on Bitcoin but didn't have the pull to do so and thus developed his own coin. Essentially, it uses less power to mine Dash than most coins. Using less energy to mine is important because mining coins is one of the most wasteful processes you can imagine. The wasteful mining process key to security and stability of all coins that use a "proof-of-work" system (it prevents people from mining too fast), but environmentally, it's kind of a nightmare. Anyway, people know what a Darkcoin is... hopefully this familiarity rolls over to Dash. Currently Dash can be exchanged for about $2.50 – $3.00 making it one of the more valuable coins in circulation.

• **Nxt**: Not only does this nifty coin sport the name of Steve Job's other company, it actually uses a really cool and totally different algorithm for producing coins. This algorithm – an implementation of a proof-of-stake scheme rather than proof-of-work – is arguably less burdensome on the environment and has long-term potential. It may be worth a tad less than the other coins we recommend being worth about a penny on the dollar on a good day, but less cost per coin means you have less to lose if the coin value deflates.

• **Peercoin**: Like Nxt, Peercoin (abbreviated PPC) uses a proof-of-stake system; in fact, it was the first proof-of-stake coin. It's worth about $0.40 on the USD and has a market cap of almost ten million. This coin has everything going for it and is a fairly smart bet as far as cryptocurrency goes. As an added bonus to confidence and quality behind the coin, Peercoin was developed by Sunny King. Sunny King is maybe-the the guy who created Bitcoin, or this other coin, or maybe Bruce Wayne or Clark Kent or something... It's hard to tell as the culture of cryptocurrency puts importance on peer-to-peer, code, and coin over developers. Still he is important and like-it-or-not little things like this could be the deciding factor between a coin sinking or swimming in the new market.

Note: In most cases, you'll have a hard time trading anything other than Bitcoin for actual money. You can trade most coins at online cryptocurrency exchanges and you can use some coins to buy certain things online. Just because a coin has a value in USD doesn't mean that anyone is going to give you USD or pay that rate for your coins. This is more like selling stocks or trading one baseball card for another then actually having money on hand. So, keep that and the volatility of the markets and coins in mind when investing.

Advice: As a rule of thumb, don't acquire any volatile assets you can't afford to lose. This is a valuable guideline for investments in general. It's really important to look at the history of the value of Bitcoin. In late 2013 / early 2014 Bitcoin gained big Media attention and the price of all coins inflated wildly and unreasonably. Since then most coins have leveled back out at about double their pre-2014 value, but there is still plenty of room to go down... of course history has shown us there is plenty of room to go up too. $1,200 Bitcoins? It could happen again.

Conceptualizing the cryptocurrency system in a nutshell:

• Electronic money.

• Mined by individuals who use their own resources to find the coins.

• A stable, finite system of currency. For example, there are only 21,000,000 Bitcoins produced for all time.

• Does not require any government or bank to make it work.

• Pricing is decided by the amount of the coins found and used which is combined with the demand from the public to possess them.

• There are several forms of crypto currency, with Bitcoin being first and foremost.

• Can bring great wealth, but, like any investment, has risks.

BITCOIN

The cryptocurrency that continues to mesmerize
the world, the first of its kind, Bitcoin was once
entirely a classy realm of tech-geniuses who were
keen to uphold the philosophy of maximizing
autonomy, but Bitcoin has a shot to fame with the
promise of a wide consumer base. Yet, to the
uninitiated consumers, a query remains. So, exactly
what is Bitcoin? Some are really yet to unravel this
overly fluctuating cryptocurrency. Generated and
stored electronically, Bitcoin is actually a form of
digital currency. The network can't actually be
controlled by anyone, the currency is
decentralized. It came into being in 2009, as a
brainchild of an individual with the assumed name
of Satoshi Nakamoto. Utilizing the P2P technology
to function, Bitcoin has the distinctive and flexible
feature to engulf anyone who's interested. Its
worldwide acceptance is a feature that adds to its
popularity.

With no accountability to anyone, Bitcoins are
fairly unique. Bitcoins are sovereign with their
distinct rules, and aren't printed in a clandestine
manner by any bank but mined, they're produced
digitally by a good number of people involved in a
colossal network or community. Miners usually

employ enormous computing power, and a great deal of competition is involved in Bitcoin mining. Computers work to solve complex mathematical problems. The competing miners also have a prospect to earn Bitcoins in the process, by just solving the problem. Although, difficulty levels of these problems are becoming intense day by day. Transactions at the Bitcoin network are relentless and incessant, and keeping track of those transactions is fairly systematic. Bitcoin network keeps it methodical, as during a given time span, all transactions are collected in a block. The miners are supposed to validate transactions, and everything is listed in a general ledger, which is simply a collection of blocks, termed as blockchain. Blockchain actually holds the key to the details of any transaction made across various Bitcoin addresses.

Bitcoin integration into people's lives is the most coveted thing right now. This is achieved quite easily by the emergence of exchanges. Bitcoin enthusiasts can have a great deal of choices when they are looking to acquire this digital currency. A Bitcoin exchange enables consumers to buy or sell Bitcoins by making use of fiat currencies. Exchanges are in abundance, but initially Mt. Gox was the most reputed and extensively used, prior to its collapse. With exchanges, consumers can purchase or sell Bitcoins with wired transfers, cash or credit/debit card payment. A real-time as well as secure trading platform is offered by the exchanges. Enthusiasm and a relentless frenzy always accompanies Bitcoins. With numerous enthusiasts who are keen to trade Bitcoins, the young currency and all the craze surrounding it seems to grow a little bit every day. All the knowledge associated with it seems to be as important as the currency itself. The significance of a "Bitcoin wiki", an autonomous project, cannot be denied at all. It will act as a storehouse of knowledge for Bitcoin enthusiasts all around the world.

Just like any other innovation, Bitcoin enjoys the support of many followers who are crazy about this idea. They love it so much that they spread it all around and even took it to another level. Indeed, Bitcoin enjoys the support of many enthusiasts and it can really prove to shape a fantastic future in terms of finance, especially since it gives the power of money back to the people and not to a central control.

The Bitcoin currency is definitely here to stay and it is not a simple trend. Everyone is looking for ways to improve Bitcoin in terms of equipment and ways of work. The exchanges are putting everything they have in the efficacy and the safety of this system. Many entrepreneurs take a chance and build their businesses around this idea. The venture capital funds support projects that are connected to Bitcoin

Bitcoin has the power to become a great force in the financial industry. The scenarios are numerous, and they all seem to support the idea that Bitcoin will retain its value, even if the fiat currency of a weak central government is consumed by hyperinflation. And we shouldn't fall into a pessimistic mood, even if there are some recorded cases of people selling valuable items in order to buy Bitcoins. All things considered, the Bitcoin monetary system can easily coexist with the traditional currencies existent in the world.

Bitcoin has injected itself into a lot of conversations about the future of technology, economics, and the internet. The future of digital currencies remains a controversial topic. After reading these 10 things to know about the confusing world of digital currencies, you'll feel confident joining the conversation.

ABOUT THE BITCOIN MARKET

Bitcoin is the digital currency that is used to buy a variety of goods and services all over the world. It works in exactly the same way as paper money but there are some key differences between the two. Bitcoin also exists in physical form but it's available in digital, the primary form meant for online trading by using wallet software or any other online service. Bitcoins can be obtained through mining or by trading other forms of money or even some goods and services.

Successful Bitcoin Marketing often results from innovative businesses simply accepting payments to open up new niches. Many businesses have had great fortunes with using Bitcoin, which further strengthens the economy by giving more uses for the cryptocurrency. The almost non-existent fees and the inability to reverse transactions is a huge selling point for business, where traditional payment methods (like credit cards) could leave the business with losses.

The Bitcoin Market

The Bitcoin market is the market where Bitcoins are traded. When you have Bitcoins, you can use them for purchasing almost anything for which this currency is accepted. There are certain kinds of trades for which Bitcoins are the only form of payment that is widely accepted. If you want to acquire that specific good, then Bitcoins will be required to complete the transaction.

Here are some of the businesses that have had great success with accepting Bitcoin as a payment method.

Bees Brothers

Bees Brothers was a business set up by three brothers that were learning about bees through farming honey. Over time, they ended up with more honey than they knew what to do with, and started to sell it locally. This eventually led to accepting Bitcoin for online purchases, being that it has no fees and is a very safe method for accepting payments (with no charge-backs), and their business exploded from there.

It is really safe to say that Bitcoin is what made their business as successful as it is today, and they, in turn, helped strengthen Bitcoin by accepting it. It is a win-win for everyone.

Expedia

Expedia is a major site for booking travel, and they have recently started accepting Bitcoin as a payment method. They tout over 290,000 bookable properties. As of yet, airline tickets and car rentals are not able to be paid via Bitcoin, but they have stated that they are working on it. It is not clear exactly how much the acceptance of Bitcoin has affected Expedia, but they stated that they came up with their own estimates as to what they should expect. Expedia further stated that they have been meeting and exceeding those estimates, leading to great things for the company (and Bitcoin).

Dell

Dell is a major computer company that pretty much everyone should already be familiar with. Their acceptance of Bitcoin was a sign that it was going to make it mainstream, or at least gain more attention from those that otherwise are uncomfortable with the idea of cryptocurrencies.

It's hard to say exactly how their business accepting the coins is going to affect them, but it is important to take into consideration the fact that their clients largely include computer experts and other knowledgeable people. In other words, it's hard to go wrong with accepting Bitcoin as a technology company.

As of yet, no information has been released as to what effects the move to accepting Bitcoin has had on Dell, though it is safe to assume it is going to at least be helpful. Even if the sales for the business don't increase, every sale that happens through Bitcoin means less money is lost due to fees and fraud.

When you step into the Bitcoin market, the first thing you need to learn is how to acquire Bitcoins. The first option is to purchase them. It will take little effort to do it this way. The second option is to mine them. Mining takes place on software that performs certain mathematical equations for which the trader is rewarded some Bitcoins. This is quite time taking and many traders say that it bears a small portion of fruit.

Process of Purchasing Bitcoins

In order to become a part of the Bitcoin market, you will need wallet software. You can also get an online service instead. There are online wallet services available in all major countries so you will not face any trouble in setting up your wallet account.

You will have to link your wallet to your bank account to let the purchasing begin. This can take a few days depending upon your wallet service.

Once your bank account is linked, you will see a buy Bitcoins link in the software window. This is going to be simple. Once the transaction is completed, the Bitcoins will be transferred to your wallet.

The Bitcoin market works on the same strategies that are used in any other type of trading market. When the price of Bitcoins becomes low, it's a signal to buy them. When the price becomes high, you can sell them to earn profit.

Mining can be hard, but all traders should still try it from time to time. It is a bit slow and so you will have to be patient. You will need Bitcoin mining software. There are even mining pools. You have to simply decrypt a block with the joint effort of a mining group. You will then get Bitcoins according to your contribution.

Keep in mind, the value of Bitcoins goes up and down within seconds. If you don't make the right move at the right time, you can lose a significant portion of your investment. A good thing is that once you fully understand the basics, you can reap lots of profits from this form of trading.

THE FUTURE OF BITCOIN

When the digital currency Bitcoin came to life in January 2009, it was noticed by almost no one apart from the handful of programmers who followed cryptography discussion groups. Its origins were shadowy: it had been conceived the previous year by a still-mysterious person or group known only by the alias Satoshi Nakamoto1. And its purpose seemed quixotic: Bitcoin was to be a 'cryptocurrency', in which strong encryption algorithms were exploited in a new way to secure transactions. Users' identities would be shielded by pseudonyms. Records would be completely decentralized. And no one would be in charge — not governments, not banks, not even Nakamoto.

Yet the idea caught on. Today, there are some 14.6 million Bitcoin units in circulation. They have a collective market value of around US$3.4 billion. Some of this growth is attributable to criminals taking advantage of the anonymity for drug trafficking and worse. But the system is also drawing interest from financial institutions such as JP Morgan Chase, which think it could streamline their internal payment processing and cut international transaction costs. It has inspired the creation of some 700 other cryptocurrencies. And on 15 September, Bitcoin officially came of age in academia with the launch of Ledger.

What fascinates academics and entrepreneurs alike is the innovation at Bitcoin's core. Known as the block chain, it serves as the official online ledger of every Bitcoin transaction, dating back to the beginning. It is also the data structure that allows those records to be updated with minimal risk of hacking or tampering — even though the block chain is copied across the entire network of computers running Bitcoin software, and the owners of those computers do not necessarily know or trust one another.

Many people see this block-chain architecture as the template for a host of other applications, including self-enforcing contracts and secure systems for online voting and crowdfunding. This is the goal of Ethereum, a block-chain-based system launched in July by the non-profit Ethereum Foundation, based in Baar, Switzerland. And it is the research agenda of the Initiative for CryptoCurrencies and Contracts (IC3), an academic consortium also launched in July, and led by Cornell University in Ithaca, New York.

Nicolas Courtois, a cryptographer at University College London, says that the Bitcoin block chain could be "the most important invention of the twenty-first century" — if only Bitcoin were not constantly shooting itself in the foot.

Several shortcomings have become apparent in Bitcoin's implementation of the block-chain idea. Security, for example, is far from perfect: there have been more than 40 known thefts and seizures of bitcoins, several incurring losses of more than $1 million apiece.

Cryptocurrency firms and researchers are attacking the problem with tools such as game theory and advanced cryptographic methods. "Cryptocurrencies are unlike many other systems, in that extremely subtle mathematical bugs can have catastrophic consequences," says Ari Juels, co-director of IC3. "And I think when weaknesses surface there will be a need to appeal to the academic community where the relevant expertise resides."

Academic interest in cryptocurrencies and their predecessors goes back at least two decades, with much of the early work spearheaded by cryptographer David Chaum. While working at the National Research Institute for Mathematics and Computer Science in Amsterdam, the Netherlands, Chaum wanted to give buyers privacy and safety. So in 1990 he founded one of the earliest digital currencies, DigiCash, which offered users anonymity through cryptographic protocols of his own devising.

DigiCash went bankrupt in 1998 — partly because it had a centralized organization akin to a traditional bank, yet never managed to fit in with the financial industry and its regulations. But aspects of its philosophy re-emerged ten years later in Nakamoto's design for Bitcoin. That design also incorporated crowdsourcing and peer-to-peer networking — both of which help to avoid centralized control. Anyone is welcome to participate: it is just a matter of going online and running the open-source Bitcoin software. Users' computers form a network in which each machine is home to one constantly updated copy of the block chain.

Nakamoto's central challenge with this wide-open system was the need to make sure that no one could find a way to rewrite the ledger and spend the same bitcoins twice — in effect, stealing bitcoins. His solution was to turn the addition of new transactions to the ledger into a competition: an activity that has come to be known as mining.

Digital currencies:

The printing press caused a revolution in its time, hailed as a democratic force for good by many. Books available to the masses was indeed a revolution; and now we also have e-books and technological devices to read them with. The fact that the original words have been encoded into a numerical form and decoded back to words electronically does not mean we trust less the words we are reading, but we may still prefer the aesthetics of a physical book than a piece of high-tech plastic which needs to have its battery charged to keep working. Can digital currencies such as bitcoin really provide a contribution to positive social change in a spectacular way?

To answer this we must ask what of money, how are we to understand it, use it and incorporate it into a sustainable model of a 'better world for all?' Money, unlike any other form of property, is unique in that it may be used for anything prior to an event even occurring. It implies nothing, yet can be used for great good or great evil, and yet it is only what it is despite its many manifestations and consequences. It is a unique but much misunderstood and misused commodity. Money has the simplicity of facilitating buying and selling, and a mathematical complexity as demonstrated by the financial markets; and yet it has no notion of egalitarianism, moral or ethical decision making. It acts as an autonomous entity, yet it is both endogenous and exogenous to the global community. It has no personality and is easily replaceable, yet it is treated as a finite resource in the global context, its growth governed by a set of complex rules which determine the way in which it may behave. Yet despite this the outcomes are never completely predictable and, furthermore; a commitment to social justice and an aversion to moral turpitude is not a requirement of its use.

In order for a currency to effectively perform the financial functions required of it, the intrinsic-value of money has to be a commonly held belief by those who use it. In November 2013 the US Senate Committee on Homeland Security & Governmental Affairs acknowledged that virtual currencies are a legitimate means of payment, an example of such is Bitcoin. Due to the very low transaction fees charged by the 'Bitcoin network' it offers a very real way to allow the transfer of funds from migrant workers sending money back to their families without having to pay high transfer fees currently charged by companies. A European Commission calculated that if the global average remittance of 10% were reduced to 5% (the '5x5' initiative endorsed by the G20 in 2011), this could result in an additional US$ 17 billion flowing into developing countries; the use of the blockchain would reduce these fees near to zero. These money transfer companies who extract wealth from the system may become dis-intermediated through the use of such an infrastructure.

Probably the most important point to note about cryptocurrencies is the distributed and decentralised nature of their networks. With the growth of the Internet, we are perhaps just seeing the 'tip of the iceberg' in respect of future innovations which may exploit undiscovered potential for allowing decentralisation but at a hitherto unseen or unimaginable scale. Thus, whereas in the past, when there was a need for a large network it was only achievable using a hierarchical structure; with the consequence of the necessity of surrendering the 'power' of that network to a small number of individuals with a controlling interest. It might be said that Bitcoin represents the decentralisation of money and the move to a simple system approach. Bitcoin represents as significant an advancement as peer-to-peer file sharing and internet telephony (Skype for example).

There is very little explicitly produced legal regulation for digital or virtual currencies, however there are a wide range of existing laws which may apply depending on the country's legal financial framework for: Taxation, Banking and Money Transmitting Regulation, Securities Regulation, Criminal and/or civil law, Consumer Rights/Protection, Pensions Regulation, Commodities and stocks regulation, and others. So the two key issues facing bitcoin are whether it can be considered as legal tender, and if as an asset then it is classed as property. It is common practice for nation-states to explicitly define currency as legal tender of another nation-state (e.g. US$), preventing them from recognising other 'currencies' formally as currency. A notable exception to this is Germany which allows for the concept of a 'unit of account' that can therefore be used as a form of 'private money' and can be used in 'multilateral clearing circles. In the other circumstance of being considered as property the obvious discrepancy here is that, unlike property, digital currencies have the capacity of divisibility into much smaller amounts. Developed, open economies are generally permissive to digital currencies. The USA has issued the most guidance and is highly represented on the map below. Capital controlled economies are effectively by definition contentious or hostile. As for many African and a few other countries the topic has not yet been addressed.

Starting from the principles of democratic participation it is immediately apparent that bitcoin does not satisfy the positive social impact component of such an objective in so far as its value is not one it can exert influence over but is subject to market-forces. However any 'new' crypto-currency may offer democratic participation when the virtual currency has different rules of governance and issuance based upon more socially based democratic principles.

So what if a "digital" currency could provide a valid alternative to existing forms of money in performing the role of contributing positively to: the goals of promoting a socially inclusive culture, the equality of opportunity and the promotion of mutualism; which as their very name implies are alternative and/or complementary to an official or national sovereign currency? Virtual cryptocurrencies such as bitcoin are a new and emerging dynamic in the system; though in their infancy, the pace of innovation in the field of cryptocurrencies had been dramatic.

There are many factors which determine the 'effectiveness' of money to bring about positive social and environmental change; pervading political ideology, economic environment, the desire of local communities and individuals to pursue alternative social outcomes whilst seeking to maximise economic opportunity, building of social capital, and many others. If a local digital currency could be designed to build extra resilience into a local economy and improve economic outcomes then, introduction on a more widespread basis merits investigation. When the current economic system fails to deliver it is manifested in such ways as: increased social isolation, higher crime rates, physical dereliction, poor health, a lack of a sense of community, amongst other undesirable social impacts.

ADVANTAGES OF BITCOIN

A few of the benefits brought by Bitcoin are seen in effective markets. A Bitcoin can be divided into millions of parts (every part is called satoshi); the fiat currency is normally broken down in hundreds). The transactions in this network are free, or in some cases include a tiny transaction fee in order to induce the miners. But we are speaking of approximately a tenth of one percent. If you are to compare this with a two or four percent fee that is generally charged by the credit card companies, you will understand why this concept is so attractive.

If you want to participate in this economy, you do not have to be a technical expert or to know too much about the subject. There are a couple of services that can be employed in order to transform the process of turning from a newbie into an experienced investor into a smooth one. Take this chance and make it work!

Critics state that using Bitcoins is unsafe because -

• They have no authentic value

• They are not regulated

• They can be used to make illegal transactions

Reasons why it is worth using Bitcoins.

1. Quick payments - When payments are made by using banks, the transaction takes some days, similarly wire transfers also take a long time. On the other hand, virtual currency Bitcoin transactions are generally more rapid.

"Zero-confirmation" transactions are instantaneous, where the merchant accepts the risk, which is still not approved by Bitcoin block-chain. If the merchant needs an approval, then the transaction takes 10 minutes. This is much more rapid than any inter-banking transfer.

2. Inexpensive - Credit or debit card transactions are instant, but you are charged a fee for using this privilege. In the Bitcoin transactions, the fees are usually low, and in some cases, it is free.

3. No one can take it away - Bitcoin is decentralized, so no central authority can take away percentage from your deposits.

4. No chargeback - Once you trade Bitcoins, they are gone. You cannot reclaim them without the recipient's consent. Thus, it becomes difficult to commit the chargeback fraud, which is often experienced by people with credit cards. People purchase goods and if they find it defective, they contact credit cards agency to make a chargeback,

effectively reversing the transaction. The credit card company does it and charges you with costly chargeback fee ranging from $5-$15.

5. Safe personal details - Credit card numbers get stolen during online payments. A Bitcoin transaction does not need any personal details. You will need to combine your private key and the Bitcoin key together to do a transaction.

6. Eliminates fraud risk - Only the Bitcoin owner can send payment to the intended recipient, who is the only one who can receive it. The network knows the transfer has occurred and transactions are validated; they cannot be challenged or taken back. This is big for online merchants who are often subject to credit card processors' assessments of whether or not a transaction is fraudulent, or businesses that pay the high price of credit card chargebacks.

7. Data is secure - As we have seen with recent hacks on national retailers' payment processing systems, the Internet is not always a secure place for private data. With Bitcoin, users do not give up private information.

a. They have two keys - a public key that serves as the bitcoin address and a private key with personal data.

b. Transactions are "signed" digitally by combining the public and private keys; a mathematical function is applied and a certificate is generated proving the user initiated the transaction. Digital signatures are unique to each transaction and cannot be re-used.

c. The merchant/recipient never sees your secret information (name, number, physical address) so it's somewhat anonymous but it is traceable (to the bitcoin address on the public key).

8. Convenient payment system -- Merchants can use Bitcoin entirely as a payment system; they do not have to hold any Bitcoin currency since Bitcoin can be converted to dollars. Consumers or merchants can trade in and out of Bitcoin and other currencies at any time.

9. International payments - Bitcoin is used around the world; e-commerce merchants and service providers can easily accept international payments, which open up new potential marketplaces for them.

10. Easy to track -- The network tracks and permanently logs every transaction in the Bitcoin

block chain (the database). In the case of possible wrongdoing, it is easier for law enforcement officials to trace these transactions.

11. Micropayments are possible - Bitcoins can be divided down to one one-hundred-millionth, so running small payments of a dollar or less becomes a free or near-free transaction. This could be a real boon for convenience stores, coffee shops, and subscription-based websites (videos, publications).

12. No Taxation- When you make purchases via dollars, euros or any other government fiat currency, you have to pay an addition sum of money to the government as tax. Every purchasable item has its own designated tax rate. However, when you're making a purchase through Bitcoin, sales taxes are not added to your purchase. This is deemed as a legal form of tax evasion and is one of the major advantages of being a Bitcoin user.

With zero tax rates, Bitcoin can come in handy especially when purchasing luxury items that are exclusive to a foreign land. Such items, more often than not, are heavily taxed by the government.

13. Flexible Online Payments- Bitcoin is an online payment system and just like any other such system, the users of Bitcoin have the luxury of paying for their coins from any corner of the world that has an internet connection. This means that

you could be lying on your bed and purchasing coins instead of taking the pain of travelling to a specific bank or store to get your work done.

Moreover, an online payment via Bitcoin does not require you to fill in details about your personal information. Hence, processing Bitcoin transactions is a lot simpler than those carried out through U.S. Bank accounts and credit cards.

14. Concealed User Identity- All Bitcoin transactions are discrete, or in other words Bitcoin gives you the option of User anonymity. Bitcoins are similar to cash only purchases in the sense that your transactions can never be tracked back to you and these purchases are never connected with your personal identity. As a matter of fact, the Bitcoin address that is created for user purchases is never the same for two different transactions.

If you want to, you do have the option of voluntarily revealing and publishing your Bitcoin transactions but in most cases users keep their identities secret.

15. No outside interventions- One of the greatest advantages of Bitcoin is that it eliminates third party interruptions. This means that governments, banks and other financial intermediaries have no authority whatsoever to disrupt user transactions or freeze a Bitcoin account. As mentioned before,

Bitcoin is based strictly on a peer to peer system. Hence, the users of Bitcoin enjoy greater liberty when making purchases with Bitcoins than they do when using conventional national currencies.

BITCOIN IN THE RETAIL ENVIRONMENT

Digital currencies such as the Bitcoin are comparatively new and haven't yet been put through major tests. As a result, many feel that there are certain risks involved in the usage of Bitcoin. Regardless of the potential disadvantages of Bitcoin, it's evident that its merits are strong enough to make it a legitimate contender to challenge conventional currencies in the not so distant future.

At checkout, the payer uses a smartphone app to scan a QR code with all the transaction information needed to transfer the bitcoin to the retailer. Tapping the "Confirm" button completes the transaction. If the user doesn't own any Bitcoin, the network converts dollars in his account into the digital currency.

The retailer can convert that Bitcoin into dollars if it wants to, there were no or very low processing fees (instead of 2 to 3 percent), no hackers can steal personal consumer information, and there is no risk of fraud.

Bitcoins in hospitality

Hotels can accept Bitcoin for room and dining payments on the premises for guests who wish to pay by Bitcoin using their mobile wallets, or PC-to-website to pay for a reservation online. A third-party BTC merchant processor can assist in handling the transactions which it clears over the Bitcoin network. These processing clients are installed on tablets at the establishments' front desk or in the restaurants for users with BTC smartphone apps. (These payment processors are also available for desktops, in retail POS systems, and integrated into foodservice POS systems.) No credit cards or money need to change hands.

These cashless transactions are fast and the processor can convert bitcoins into currency and make a daily direct deposit into the establishment's bank account. It was announced in January 2014 that two Las Vegas hotel-casinos will accept Bitcoin payments at the front desk, in their restaurants, and in the gift shop.

Bitcoins for International Travel

The phenomenon of bitcoins has taken over the financial and business world by storm. In a world whereconvenience is put at a premium, most people want to deal with something handy and avoid too much hassle. Being a virtual currency, bitcoins have gradually started replacing the bulky traditional bank notes and cheques. Businesses and banks are conducting awareness campaigns for their customers to take up this mode of payment, as it is stress free and time-saving. The main advantage is that you can track past transactions and exchange rates on a Bitcoin Chart. The following are further reasons why you should put bitcoins in your list of must-haves:

Universal

When you are travelling, the process of exchanging currency is quite cumbersome. This is especially worse when you are going to more than one destination. In addition, carrying large amounts of cash is not only tiresome but also risky. Bitcoins give you the comfort of carrying as much money as you need in a virtual state. It is common among traders all over the world and hence saves you the inconvenience of dealing with more than one currency.

Less costly

When you trade using cash, you are subject to abrupt price changes in essential commodities. You end up spending much more than you had budgeted because of punitive exchange rates. Bitcoins is a global currency that has stable rates and value, and will save you the time and high fees.

Secure

Bitcoins is fraud proof due to the heavy cryptography that goes into its making. There are no incidences of hacking or leaking of people's personal information. When you use the conventional money transfer methods abroad, you are likely to fall into the hands of hackers who might infiltrate your bank accounts. With bitcoins, you alone have access to your account and can authorize any money into and from it.

Irreversible

As a seller, you have probably experienced a situation where a client reverses an already complete transaction. Bitcoins protect you from such incidences, as these transfers cannot be reversed. You should be careful with your bitcoins to avoid transferring them to a wrong person.

Convenient

Unlike normal banks that require proof of identification to open an account, bitcoins allows anyone to access it without asking for proof. Transactions are instant and are not limited by geographical boundaries or time zones, and there is no paperwork involved. To join bitcoins, you only need to download the bitcoin wallet and create an account.

WHAT BITCOIN CAN BE USED FOR?

Practically, almost any product or service that can be bought with dollars or other currencies can also be bought with bitcoins. On the other hand, the high volatility of bitcoins is a huge risk for some people that might want to use this cryptocurrency, but they are afraid about price differences. Even so, the characteristics of bitcoins make them perfect for internet payments:

1. Fast transactions

A bitcoin transaction is processed in 10-15 minutes. In case of a bank transfer, it might take hours or even days for the money to get from one account to the other. Some might say that PayPal or other ewallets are even faster. It is true, but there are other aspects that ewallets can't give: privacy and smaller commissions.

2. Privacy

When you send bitcoins to a partner over the internet, the transaction will be registered in a blockchain. The list of transactions is public, and it can be verified on specialized websites. Only the identification number, the sum and the time are recorded. There is no way for somebody to find out from where the bitcoins come, and where they go. This characteristic of bitcoins attracted many people. Well, some of those are interested about it because they can buy illegal goods with it , but the majority of bitcoin users are people that want to buy legal items and services, but which don't want to disclose their identity. Porn and gambling websites might be immoral, but they are not illegal, so people that want to subscribe for those services can safely pay in bitcoins on the websites that accept this currency, knowing that their reputation will not be affected.

3. Smaller commissions

The average commission is 0.002 BTC for a transaction. It is significantly smaller compared with the PayPal or banking commissions. Moreover, you are not even obliged to pay it. By paying a commission, you "reserve" the computational power of a pool (or at least a part of it), to process your transaction faster. You even have the possibility not to pay the commission. In this case, you might need to wait two or even three days for your transaction to be processed. If you are not in a hurry, this might be the perfect opportunity to make money transactions with zero costs.

Of course, there are also disadvantages for using bitcoins, such as the possibility to lose them. If somebody steals your bitcoins, or if you delete the wallet files, it is impossible to recover those. As long as the bitcoin is not regulated, there is no central organism for arbitrage between divergent parts. In other words, you can't complain if you lose or get robbed of your bitcoins, simply because there is nobody to complain to.

BITCOIN DISADVANTAGES

Lack of Awareness & Understanding: Fact is, many people are still unaware of digital currencies and Bitcoin. People need to be educated about Bitcoin to be able to apply it to their lives. Networking is a must to spread the word on Bitcoin. Businesses are accepting bitcoins because of the advantages, but the list is relatively small compared to physical currencies.

Companies like Tigerdirect and Overstock accepting Bitcoin as payment is great. However, if they do not have a knowledgeable staff that understands digital currencies, how will they help customers understand and use Bitcoin for transactions?

The workers need to be educated on Bitcoin so that they can help the customers. This will definitely take some time and effort. Otherwise, what is the benefit of such large companies accepting Bitcoin if its staff doesn't even know what digital currencies are?

Risk and Volatility: Bitcoin has volatility mainly due to the fact that there is a limited amount of coins and the demand for them increases by each passing day. However, it is expected that the volatility will decrease as more time goes on.

As more businesses, medias, and trading centers begin to accept Bitcoin, its' price will eventually settle down. Currently, Bitcoin's price bounces everyday mainly due to current events that are related to digital currencies.

Still Developing: Bitcoin is still at its infancy stage with incomplete features that are in development. To make the digital currency more secure and accessible, new features, tools, and services are currently being developed. Bitcoin has some growth to do before it comes to its full and final potential. This is because Bitcoin is just starting out, and it needs to work out its problems just like how any currency in its beginning stage would need to.

HOW BITCOIN ARE BEING USED FOR MINING DIGITAL CURRENCY

It is a well-known fact that bitcoin mining hardware has changed by leaps and bounds in recent times due to the evolution of new central processing units in the market. The new machines can conduct Bitcoin processing at a faster rate as compared to the computers of the past. Moreover, they consume less power and last for a very long period. Field programming gate array processors are connected with the CPUs to enhance their computing power. While selecting hardware for Bitcoin processing, make sure that it has a large hash rate that would deliver spectacular results to the users. According to the experts, the speed of the data processing is measured in mega hash rates per second or GIGA hash rates per second.

Another parameter for selecting the best bitcoin mining hardware is to analyze the power consumption of different machines available on the market. If the CPU requires lot of electricity, it can have a bad impact on the output and the business operations. Therefore, the hardware must be of high quality and cost-effective to attract the attention of the people. Expenditure on electricity bill should be in synchronization with the bitcoins earned through the application. One should take into account that CPU consumes own electricity for its operation and also requires more to power up the bitcoin mining hardware. Combined expenditure must be compared with the benefits accrued by the machine.

One of the most important components of the hardware is the graphical processing unit that can easily handle complex polygon calculations. As a result, it is quite useful in solving the issue of transaction blocks with bitcoin processing. According to the experts, GPUs have a distinct advantage over the hashing technology of CPU because of their higher processing power. Apart from handling bitcoins, GPUs can also manage the data transfer of crypto-currencies without any problem making it compatible with other applications.

ASIC option has been introduced in the market for bitcoin mining purposes because it has far more power than the graphics card. It is embedded into the motherboard of the computer along with other gates customized for achieving the processing objectives. The field programmable gate array located on the board is able to deliver a power of 750 megahashes per second. With powerful machines bitcoin can be mined at an astonishing rate. Although, the customized chips are expensive and take some time to be fabricated, the data speed provided by them is awesome.

Bitcoins - Global Impact of Virtual Currencies

The most significant characteristic of Bitcoin is that unlike conventional and traditional printed currency, it is an electronic payment system that is based on mathematical proof. Traditional currencies have centralized banking systems that control them and in the absence of any single institution controlling it, the US Treasury has termed the Bitcoin a 'decentralized virtual currency'. The underlying idea behind Bitcoin was to produce a currency entirely independent of any central authority and one that could be transferred electronically and instantly with almost nil transaction fees.

By the end of 2015, the number of merchant traders accepting Bitcoin payments for products and services exceeded 100,000. Major banking and financial regulatory authorities such as the European Banking Authority for instance have warned that users of Bitcoin are not protected by chargeback or refund rights, although financial experts in major financial centers accept that

Bitcoin can provide legitimate and valid financial services. On the other hand, the increasing use of Bitcoin by criminals has been cited by legislative authorities, law enforcement agencies and financial regulators as a major cause of concern.

The owner of Bitcoin voucher service Azteco, Akin Fernandez comments that there will shortly be an important game-changer in the manner Bitcoin is generated. The rate of Bitcoin generation every day will be literally 'halved' and this may alter the perception of Bitcoin completely, although it will be almost impossible to predict how the public at large and the merchants will react to such a move.

Against the backdrop of such a move, the predictions are that the transaction volume of Bitcoin is set to triple this year riding on the back of a probable Donald Trump presidency. Some market commentators are of the view that the price of the digital currency could spike in the event of such a possibility leading to market turmoil globally.

The Panama Papers scandal which broke out in May this year has spurred the European Union to fight against tax avoidance strategies that the rich and powerful use to stash wealth by bringing in new rules. The current rules seek to close the loopholes and among the measures proposed are efforts to end anonymous trading on virtual currency platforms like Bitcoin. A lot more research has to be done by the European Banking Authority and the European Central Bank on the best strategies to deal with digital currencies as currently there is no EU legislation governing them.

Bitcoin Ransom

DDoS extortion is certainly not a new trick by the hacker community, but there have been several new developments to it. Notable among them is the use of Bitcoin as a method of payment. DD4BC (DDoS for Bitcoin) is a hacker (or hacker group) who has been found to extort victims with DdoS attacks, demanding payment via Bitcoin. DD4BC seems to focus on the gaming and payment processing industries that use Bitcoin.

In November 2014, reports emerged of the group having sent a note to the Bitalo Bitcoin exchange demanding 1 Bitcoin in return for helping the site enhance its protection against DDoS attacks. At the same time, DD4BC executed a small-scale attack to demonstrate the exchange vulnerability to this method of disruption. Bitalo ultimately refused to pay the ransom, however. Instead, the site publicly accused the group of blackmail and extortion as well as created a bounty of more than USD

$25,000 for information regarding the identities of those behind DD4BC.

The plots have several common characteristics. During these extortion acts, the hacker: Launches an initial DDoS attack (ranging from a few minutes to a few hours) to prove the hacker is able to compromise the website of the victim. Demands payment via Bitcoin while suggesting they are actually helping the site by pointing out their vulnerability to DdoS

Unprotected sites can be taken down by these attacks. A recent study by Arbor Networks concluded that a vast majority of DD4BCs actual attacks have been UDP Amplification attacks, exploiting vulnerable UDP Protocols such as NTP and SSDP. In the spectrum of cyber-attacks, UDP flooding via botnet is a relatively simple, blunt attack that simply overwhelms a network with unwanted UDP traffic. These attacks are not technically complex and are made easier with rented botnets, booters, and scripts.

The typical pattern for the DD4BC gang is to launch DDoS attacks targeting layer 3 and 4, but if this does not have the desired effect, they will/can move it to layer 7, with various types of loopback attacks with post/get requests. The initial attack typically lies on a scale between 10-20GBps. This is rather massive, but often not even close to the real threat.

If a company fails to meet their requests, and if that company does not migrate this attack through various anti-DDoS services, the group will typically move on after 24 hours of a sustained attack. But you should not count on this pattern to manage your cyber security tactics.

DDoS Protection: Automatic detection and mitigation of DDoS attacks to ensure your application stays online are always available.

Application Delivery: Having server load problems? Deliver content at lightning speed with our Application Delivery Controller.

DNS Firewall: Egress firewall for your enterprise network to prevent data exfiltration through malware.

HOW TO BUY BITCOIN

The best way to learn about bitcoin, is to jump in and get a few in your "pocket" to get a feel for how they work. Despite the hype about how difficult and dangerous it can be, getting bitcoins is a lot easier and safer than you might think. In a lot of ways, it is probably easier than opening an account at a traditional bank. And, given what has been happening in the banking system, it is probably safer too.

There are a few things to learn: getting and using a software wallet, learning how to send and receive money, learning how to buy bitcoin from a person or an exchange.

Preparation: Before getting started, you will need to get yourself a wallet. You can do this easily enough by registering with one of the exchanges which will host wallet for you. And, although I think you are going to want to have one or more exchange wallets eventually, you should start with one on your own computer both to get a better feel for bitcoin and because the exchanges are still experimental themselves. When we get to that stage of the discussion, I will be advising that you get in the habit of moving your money and coins off the exchanges or diversifying across exchanges to keep your money safe.

What is a wallet? It is a way to store your bitcoins. Specifically, it is a software that has been designed to store bitcoin. It can be run on your desktop computer, laptop, mobile device (except, as yet, Apple) and can also be made to store bitcoins on things like thumb drives. If you are concerned about being hacked, then that is a good option. Even the Winklevoss* twins, who have millions invested in bitcoin, put their investment on hard drives which they then put into a safety deposit box.

The Winklevoss twins are the ones who originally had the idea for a social networking site that became Facebook. They hired Mark Zuckerberg who took their idea as his own and became immensely rich.

What do you need to know about having a bitcoin wallet on your computer? Below you can download the original bitcoin wallet, or client, in Windows or Mac format. These are not just wallets, but are in fact part of the bitcoin network. They will receive, store, and send your bitcoins. You can create one or more addresses with a click (an address is a number that looks like this: 1LyFcQatbg4BvT9gGTz6VdqqHKpPn5QBuk). You will see a field where you can copy and paste a number like this from a person you want to send money to and off it will go directly into that person's wallet. You can even create a QR code which will let someone take a picture with an app on their phone and send you some bitcoin. It is perfectly safe to give these out - the address and QR code are both for my donations page. Feel free to donate!

NOTE: This type of wallet acts both as a wallet for you and as part of the bitcoin system. The reason bitcoin works is that every transaction is broadcast and recorded as a number across the entire system (meaning that every transaction is confirmed and made irreversible by the network itself). Any computer with the right software can be part of that system, checking and supporting the network. This wallet serves as your personal wallet and also as a support for that system. Therefore, be aware that it will take up 8-9 gigabytes of your computer's memory. After you install the wallet, it will take as much as a day for the wallet to sync with the network. This is normal, does not harm your computer, and makes the system as a whole more secure, so it's a good idea.

After you get the wallet set up, take a few minutes clicking around. Things to look for:

1. There will be a page that shows you how many bitcoins are currently in your wallet. Keep in mind that bitcoins can be broken up into smaller pieces, so you may see a decimal with a lot of zeros after it. (Interesting note, 0.00000001 is one Satoshi, named after the pseudonymous creator of bitcoin).

2. There will be an area showing what your recent transactions are.

3. There will be an area where you can create an address and a QR code (like the one I have above). You don't need the QR code if you don't want it, but if you run a business and you want to accept bitcoin, then all you'll need to do to accept payment is to show someone the QR code, let them take a picture of it, and they will be able to send you some money. You will also be able to create as many addresses as you like, so if you want to track where the money is coming from, you could have a separately labeled address from each one of your payees.

4. There will be an area with a box for you to paste a code when you want to send money to someone or to yourself on an exchange or different wallet.

There will be other options and features, but to start out with, these are the items that you should know about.

How Not to Buy Bitcoin

I am going to explain a couple of key points about buying from Bitcoin Exchanges. Before I do, let me give you a warning.

A short history lesson: When people first started setting up actual business based on bitcoin, they used all of the tools available to any merchant. They sold by credit card and PayPal. The problem with this business model was quickly spotted: bitcoin transactions are not reversible by anyone except the recipient of the money.

Credit cards and PayPal have strong buyer protection policies that make it relatively easy for people to request a chargeback. So, nefarious individuals realized this and began making purchases of bitcoin and then sooner or later requesting a chargeback. And, since bitcoin is a non-physical product, sent by new and poorly understood technological means, the sellers were not able to contest this. Because of this, sellers stopped accepting credit cards and PayPal.

This was a big problem for the currency: How to move money between buyers and seller? Some business emerged that would credit you with bitcoin if you wired them money. Very often these businesses would give addresses in Albania, Poland, or Russia. The fact is that many of these did work and there are a lot of stories on the forums of people who bought bitcoins this way. But it took a lot of time and in the meantime the buyer just had to bite his or her fingernails wondering if they would get their bitcoins or kiss their investment goodbye.

Getting Your First Bitcoins

Now that you have a wallet, you will, of course, want to test them out.

The very first place to go is http://faucet.bitcoin.st/.

This is a website that gives out small amounts of bitcoin for the purpose of getting people used to using them. The original version of this was run by the lead developer of bitcoin, Gavin Andreson. That site has since closed and this site operates by sending out one or two advertisements a month. You agree to receive those messages by requesting the bitcoins. Copy and paste your new bitcoin address and enter a phone number to which you can receive an SMS. They send out an SMS to be sure that people are not continuously coming back for more since it costs nothing to create a bitcoin address. They will also send out once or twice a month advertisement to support their operation. The amount they send it trivial: 0.0015 BTC (or 1.5 mBTC). However, they process almost immediately and you can check to see that your address and wallet are working. It is also quite a feeling to get that portion of a bitcoin. (Non-disclaimer: I have no connection with this site and receive nothing if you use them. I simply think they are a good way to get your feet wet).

Congratulations! You have just entered the bitcoin economy.

To get your feet a little wetter, you can go panning for gold. There are a number of services and websites out there that will pay you in bitcoin to do things like go to certain websites, fill out online surveys, or watch sponsored videos. These are harmless, and you can earn a few extra bitcoins this way, but it is important to remember that these are businesses that get paid when people click on the links on their sites. They are essentially kicking back a portion of what they get paid to you. There is nothing illegal, or even immoral about this (you might like what you see and make a purchase!), but they are frequently flashy and may not be completely straightforward. All the ones that I have tried (particularly bitvisitor.com) have paid out as advertised. It is interesting to experiment with these, but even with the likely rise in the value of bitcoin, you won't become a millionaire doing this. So, unless you are an advertisement junkie, I would recommend you move on. If you would like to try, simply Google "free bitcoins" or something along those lines and you will find numerous sites.

Buying Bitcoin Hand-to-Hand

Finally, this is going to be the real test of bitcoin. Can people easily trade them back and forth? If this can't happen, then there can't really be a bitcoin economy because retailers won't be able to use it. If retailers can't use it, what earthly good is it? Fortunately, this is not really a problem. iPhone is a bit of a hold out, but many smartphones have apps (mobile wallets) that will read QR codes and allow you to send bitcoin to whomever you want. You can also display a QR code of your address, or even carry a card in your wallet with your QR code to let people send bitcoin to you. Depending on what kind of wallet you have, you can then check to see if the bitcoins have been received.

A couple of things to note:

When you set up your wallet, if you click around a bit, you will see an option to pay a fee to speed transactions. This money becomes available to a bitcoin miner as he/she/they process bitcoin information. The miners doing the work of creating blocks of information keeps the system up to date and secure. The fee is an incentive to the miner to be sure to include your information in the next information block and therefore "verify" it. In the short term, miners are making most of their money by mining new coins (check the section on What Are Bitcoins for more information about this). In the long term, as it gets harder to find new coins, and as the economy increases, the fees will be an incentive for miners to keep creating more blocks and keep the economy going.

Your wallet should be set to pay 0 fees as a default, but if you want, you can add a fee to prioritize your transactions. You are under no obligation to pay a fee, and many organizations that process many small transactions (like the ones that pan for gold described above) produce enough fees to keep the miners happy.

In clicking around your wallet, on the transactions page or linked to specific transactions, you will see a note about confirmations. When you make a transaction, that information is sent out into the network and the network will send back a confirmation that there is no double entry for that bitcoin. It is smart to wait until you get several confirmations before walking away from someone who has paid you. It is actually not very easy to scam someone hand-to-hand like this, and it is not very cost-effective for the criminal, but it can be done.

Should you buy bitcoin?

As the world's current front runner in the Crypto Currency market, Bitcoin have been making some serious headlines, and some serious fluctuations in the last 6 months. Almost everyone has heard of them, and almost everyone has an opinion. Some can't fathom the idea that a currency with any value can be created from nothing, whilst some love the idea that something without Government control can be traded as a valuable entity in its own right.

Where you sit on the "Should I Buy Bitcoin?" fence probably ultimately boils down to one question: Can I Make Money from Bitcoin?

Can You Make Money from Bitcoin?

In just the last 6 months, we have seen the price go from $20 a coin in February, up to $260 a coin in April, back down to $60 in March, and back up to $130 in May. The price has now settled to around $1000 a Bitcoin, but what happens next is anyone's guess.

Bitcoin's future ultimately rests on two major variables: its adoption as a currency by a wide audience, and the absence of prohibitive Government intervention.

The Bitcoin community is growing rapidly, interest in the Crypto currency has spread dramatically online, and new services are accepting Bitcoin payments increasingly. Blogging giant, WordPress, accepts Bitcoin payments, and African based mobile application provider, Kipochi, have developed a Bitcoin wallet that will allow Bitcoin payments on mobile phones in developing nations.

We have already seen people make millions on the currency. We are seeing increasing numbers of people experimenting with living only on Bitcoin for months on end, whilst recording the experience for documentary viewing.

You can buy a takeaway in Boston, coffee in London, and even a few cars on Craigslist using

Bitcoin. Searches for Bitcoin have rocketed in 2013, with April's hike and subsequent fall in the Bitcoin price. Last week the first large acquisition of a Bitcoin company was made for SatoshiDice, an online gambling site, for 126,315 BTC (about $11.47 million), by an undisclosed buyer. This rapid growth in awareness and uptake looks set to continue, if trust in the currency remains strong. Which leads to the second dependency.

Government regulation, although specifically designed to work independently from Government control, Bitcoin will inevitably be affected by Governments in some way. This must be the case for two reasons.

Firstly, to achieve high levels of adoption, Bitcoin will have to be accessible to large numbers of people, and that means spreading beyond the realms of hidden transactions to normal everyday transactions for individuals and businesses.

Secondly, these Bitcoin transactions could become a trackable part of people's taxable wealth, to be declared and regulated alongside any other kind of wealth.

The European Union has already declared that Bitcoin is not classed as a Fiat currency, or as money, and as such, will not be regulated in its own right. In the US, the 50 state system and number of bureaucratic bodies involved has inevitably made decisions more difficult, with no consensus reached thus far. Bitcoin is not considered to be money as such, but it is considered to act like money.

A thriving Bitcoin market in the US has a more uncertain future for now, and any conclusive legislation in the US could either have a very positive, or a very negative effect on the future of Bitcoin.

So, Should You Buy Bitcoin? The answer depends mostly on how risk averse you are. Bitcoin certainly isn't going to be a smooth investment, but the potential of this currency is huge.

Important Things to Consider Before Buying Bitcoins

When the central bank in Cyprus froze bank accounts and limited the amount of cash that could be withdrawn from bank accounts it created a huge uproar that was felt around the world. If consumers did not have access to money how could they buy and sell the things needed to carry on in our modern world? The reality is, they cannot so consumers around the world started to look for safer alternatives to fiat currency. Fiat currency is currency that has no tangible value aside from what the government assigns to it.

1. Consumers are looking for a way to store their buying power to protect themselves from having bank accounts frozen for indefinite periods of time. Many people started trading in Bitcoins. This is a crypto-currency which means it cannot be easily counterfeited but before anyone starts buying into this new currency it would be prudent to understand the risks.

2. Bitcoins are not issued by any central bank or government so there is no accountability whatsoever. If you are dealing with Dollars,Euros or Pounds you have the assurance that the government behind it will honor the debt while Bitcoins do not provide any guarantees at all. The fact that no one truly knows who made this currency so there is no way of knowing whether it could be stolen right from under our eyes.

3. These Bitcoins are stored inside a digital wallet that can be encrypted on your computer. While this should provide a sense of security if your computer is lost your

Bitcoins are gone as well. It is not like a credit card where you can get a replacement and carry on like nothing has happened.

4. While the security of this currency is a concern by far the biggest worry is the value of it. The perceived value of a Bitcoin can change in a moment and unlike fiat currencies that are backed by hard assets owned by a country if a Bitcoin value drops you have nothing of value at all.

5. There are a few exchanges around the world that sell and buy Bitcoins, but you should not buy them thinking they are going to rise in value. They are a digital commodity which some would classify as a "fad". Tomorrow it could lose all its real value and never recover.

6. When it comes to investing you should never make rash decisions but weigh the risks and potential payoff and remember that there is no sure things when it comes to digital currencies like Bitcoins, so approach at your own risk.

BITCOIN AND BINARY OPTIONS TRADING

Binary options have been becoming more and more popular in the last 2 years. This type of trading has been desired among new traders as they don't need to actually buy anything, just predict whether the asset will move up or down in specified time frame. Those trades are happening in short time frames (30 sec, 1 min, 5 min) but might be months too. If the trader predicted wrongly, they will obviously lose their money. If the trader was right in his/her prediction, they will receive 80-85% payout, depending on the broker.

Binary options are sometimes referred to as 'all-or-nothing options', 'digital options', or 'fixed return options' (FROs), which are traded on the American Stock Exchange.

Bitcoin (BTC) is a digital currency which is created and held electronically and no one controls it. "Bitcoin is an online payment system invented by Satoshi Nakamoto, who published his invention in 2008, and released it as open-source software in 2009. The system is peer-to-peer; users can transact directly without needing an intermediary.Transactions are verified by network nodes and recorded in a public distributed ledger called the blockchain. The ledger uses its own unit of account, also called bitcoin. The system works without a central repository or single administrator, which has led the US Treasury to categorize it as a decentralized virtual currency. Bitcoin is often called the first cryptocurrency... "

Bitcoin as a currency in binary options trading

Bitcoin is now a widely used currency and many trading platforms accept it as a method of payment for their clients' trading deposits. There are many benefits using Bitcoin as a currency. The first benefit is "the fact that the cost of transaction is the lowest among all forms of online payment. This is the very reason why Bitcoin was created in the first place, to lower the cost of online transaction. Since there is no central authority managing Bitcoin, no service fee is paid when receiving or transmitting payment." Another reason for traders to use Bitcoin as a currency is that Bitcoin itself is tradeable and they can earn extra Bitcoins that way.

"By having all the trading transactions denoted in Bitcoin, a trader is able to shield himself from the fluctuation of this crypto currency while at the same time earn more of it through profits earned in trading."

Bitcoins for binary options trading:

The prices on the Bitcoin chart keep changing according to the supply and demand ratio. In addition to trading on the price fluctuations of this cryptocurrency, you can also use it as a mode of payment for purchasing other currencies too.

However, it is very important for you to choose a reliable binary options broker who allows you to use Bitcoins as one of their accepted currencies. You can check out the broker reviews on the rating sites, before choosing the right platforms for binary options trading.

We provide Bitcoin news and trading education resources on our website. You could also refer to the live Bitcoin chart on our website to identify the market trends and fluctuating prices.

Bitcoin as a commodity in binary options trading

With a recent popularity of Bitcoin and its acceptance as a currency, many binary options platforms started using Bitcoin as one of the currencies to trade. so as an asset. Stockbrokers are seeing the value in trading BTC against fiat currencies, mainly versus American Dollar.

Today there are 2 main types of Bitcoin binary options platforms:

• First-generation brokers - binary options platforms that allow trading on Bitcoin

• Second-generation brokers - platforms that offer both Bitcoin funding and Bitcoin trading

First generation brokers - brokers who offer Bitcoin trading:

Coinut - only Bitcoin options exchange platform; programmed as a robust and distributed on Linux operating system coinut.com

BTClevels - Bitcoin binary options trading platform; with or without registration, hassle free btclevels.com. 24 Options - one of the first brokers who started offering BTC as an asset 24option.com

Second-generation brokers - brokers who offer Bitcoin funding and trading:

Traderush binary platform - accepts BTC deposits traderush.com

Nadex trading platform -accepts BTC funding and allows BTC trading; offers limited risk, short-term

trading, transparency and full regulated market
nadex.com

Satoshi Option trading platform - accepts BTC
funding and allows BTC trading; doesn't require
account registration neither personal details.
Payouts are near instantaneous and the service is
accessible from anywhere in the world
satoshioption.com

BTCOracle platform - Bitcoin only platform -
allows BTC funding and trading offering few
wallet options and full transparency btcoracle.com

Bitstamp platform - As above, BTC only platform -
allows BTC trading and funding but requires login
bitstamp.net

Bitcoin Wisdom - allows trading 3 digital
currencies, Bitcoins, Litecoins, Altcoins versus
other fiat currencies and requires login
bitcoinwisdom.com

Beast Option - allows BTC funding and trading of
Bitcoins and Litecoins; guarantees fairness in
pricing regardless of market fluctuations
beastoptions.com

When choosing a Bitcoin broker it is important to
check their terms and conditions, paying a
particular attention to the information whether

their Bitcoin Assets are stored in "Deep Cold Storage". It means that Bitcoins are insured and stored offline, where they are not susceptible to hackers.

Differences between Bitcoin and traditional currencies (e.g. U.S. dollar):

Bitcoin does not have a centralized authority or clearing house (e.g. government, central bank, MasterCard or Visa network). The peer-to-peer payment network is managed by users and miners around the world. The currency is anonymously transferred directly between users through the internet without going through a clearing house. This means that transaction fees are much lower.

Bitcoin is created through a process called "Bitcoin mining". Miners around the world use mining software and computers to solve complex bitcoin algorithms and to approve Bitcoin transactions. They are awarded with transaction fees and new Bitcoins generated from solving Bitcoin algorithms.

There is a limited amount of Bitcoins in circulation. According to Blockchain, there were about 12.1 million in circulation as of Dec. 20, 2013. The difficulty to mine Bitcoins (solve algorithms) becomes harder as more Bitcoins are generated, and the maximum amount in circulation is capped at 21 million. The limit will not be reached until approximately the year 2140. This makes Bitcoins more valuable as more people use them.

A public ledger called 'Blockchain' records all Bitcoin transactions and shows each Bitcoin owner's respective holdings. Anyone can access the public ledger to verify transactions. This makes the digital currency more transparent and predictable. More importantly, the transparency prevents fraud and double spending of the same Bitcoins.

The digital currency can be acquired through Bitcoin mining or Bitcoin exchanges.

The digital currency is accepted by a limited number of merchants on the web and in some brick-and-mortar retailers.

 Bitcoin wallets (similar to PayPal accounts) are used for storing Bitcoins, private keys and public addresses as well as for anonymously transferring Bitcoins between users.

Bitcoins are not insured and are not protected by government agencies. Hence, they cannot be recovered if the secret keys are stolen by a hacker or lost to a failed hard drive, or due to the closure of a Bitcoin exchange. If the secret keys are lost, the associated Bitcoins cannot be recovered and would be out of circulation.

I believe that Bitcoin will gain more acceptance from the public because users can remain anonymous while buying goods and services online, transactions fees are much lower than credit card payment networks; the public ledger is accessible by anyone, which can be used to prevent fraud; the currency supply is capped at 21 million, and the payment network is operated by users and miners instead of a central authority.

However, I do not think that it is a great investment vehicle because it is extremely volatile and is not very stable. For example, the bitcoin price grew from around $14 to a peak of $1,025 USD this year before dropping to $820 per BTC at the time of writing.

Bitcoin surged this year because investors speculated that the currency would gain wider acceptance and that it would increase in price. The currency plunged 50% in December because BTC China (China's largest Bitcoin operator) announced that it could no longer accept new deposits due to government regulations. And according to Bloomberg, the Chinese central bank barred financial institutions and payment companies from handling bitcoin transactions.

Bitcoin will likely gain more public acceptance over time, but its price is extremely volatile and very sensitive to news-such as government regulations and restrictions-that could negatively impact the currency.

Understanding Why Bitcoin Is Gaining Popularity in the Binary Options Trading

It uses peer-to-peer technology, and is not controlled by any central authorities. The transactions are carried out collectively among the involved parties and the network, without any intervention from the central banks. It is free from any kind of interferences or manipulations by the governments, since it is totally decentralized.

It is solely a digital form of currency, and you cannot replace them with their physical form. However, you can quickly exchange them for dollars anytime you like.

The top cap of issuing Bitcoins is limited to 21 millions, which is an average of just 25 coins being mined for every 10 minutes. The pace of mining has slowed down even more in the last 2 years.

Bitcoins has limitations in acceptance, because they are not universally accepted at all stores. However, the prospect of acceptance does look better with its growing popularity. This cryptocurrency has come a long way since its introduction in 2009.

Bitcoins are a bit more complex to understand when compared to the conventional currencies like dollars. Therefore, you will need to gain some technical knowledge about them, especially before using them for online trading

One of the drawbacks of Bitcoins is that the transactions will generally take around 10 minutes to complete, which is unlike the regular currencies where the transactions can be completed immediately. Also, the transactions are irreversible, and the refunding can be done only if the recipient agrees to do so.

Bitcoin allows you to make transactions in an anonymous manner, because you will not have to give your name or address. Like mentioned above, it works with the peer-to-peer system.

Before buying Bitcoins, you will need to install the Bitcoin wallet, on your smartphone or computer. In addition to computer and mobile wallets, you can go for the online wallet too. Each wallet will have a specific address code. For each transaction, 2 pair of keys (public and private) will be generated. This encryption system is very secure.

The Bitcoin balance of each account is public, which means anyone can know about the balance of a particular wallet. However, you will still stay anonymous, because you don't have to give your name or private information for doing transactions.

These days many of the Forex and binary options trading brokers has started accepting Bitcoin as one of the currencies. You can buy and sell it against regular currencies like dollars and pounds.

THE IMPACT OF BITCOIN ON CURRENCY

Bitcoin is a revolutionary kind of currency that was introduced in 2009! It functions by enabling transactions to go through without the need for the middle man. Therefore no banks are required.

You also get the benefit of no transaction fees and no need giving out your real name. With such flexibility bitcoin has become widely accepted by both consumers and merchants. It also can be used to purchase web hosting services, foods online, and just about any service you can think of online.

Bitcoin has impacted much on the currency arena. It can be easily utilized to purchase merchandise anonymously. It also provides the benefits of easy and cheap international payments and is not subjected or limited to any country or regulation. Some people see Bitcoin as a vehicle for investments and buy Bitcoin by trusting that they will increase in value.

To get Bitcoins, you can purchase on an Exchange marketplace that allows people buy or sell them, utilizing other various currencies.The transferring of Bitcoins is easily done by forwarding Bitcoins to one another person utilizing mobile apps or their PCs online. It's just like sending cash digitally.

With Bitcoins you have a currency value that can be stored in what's called a "digital wallet," which subsists either within the cloud or on a computer. This digital wallet is like a virtual bank account that lets account holders within it send or receive Bitcoins, purchase goods and services or store them.

Although most bank accounts are insured by the FDIC, Bitcoin wallets are not, yet they are safe, secure and have payment flexibility benefits.Unlike the US dollar, gold, silver, or some other precious metals, Bitcoins are scarce and this scarcity is algorithmic.

 In terms of international remittance Bitcoin is a winner. There is no worry about fraud or security. At some money exchange businesses for instance, migrant workers could utilize Bitcoin to send payments from one nation to another via email.

On the 27th of June in 2014, the US Government was scheduled to auction off about 30,000 BTC that was confiscated from the shutdown of Silk Road, an online black market operation. At that time, the value of Bitcoins was 633.84 dollars. Today, one Bitcoin is worth about $820 US dollars.

If you take a good look at some of the local merchants downtown, the inner cities or online, you will see the Bitcoin logo acceptance in the window or on the door.

Bitcoin is still maturing and is making a tremendous progression towards being one of the most sensible currencies ever created.

HOW TO EARN BITCOIN ONLINE

Bitcoin is the world's first peer to peer crypto-currency that isn't controlled by any central issuing agency but is rather an open source protocol that is followed by all the people who participate in the economy. No one can manipulate the supply of Bitcoins and all transactions that take place in this economy are cryptographically verified through a process called Bitcoin mining. Your Bitcoins are as secure as public key cryptography can be.

Once you understand and appreciate the concept of Bitcoin, the next logical question is, how do you earn some Bitcoin? Here are some ideas -

• Make money online and convert them to Bitcoin: Believe it or not, it is still much easier to make US Dollars! You can then exchange these dollars you make for Bitcoin at any of the exchanges such as Bitstamp or Coinbase if you're located in the US.

• Earn Bitcoin Directly in the Bitcoin economy: There is a small but very vibrant community where you can do most tasks, but at a much smaller scale. For instance, you can take up a part-time job for Bitcoin on Coinality or you can end up with a small gig on Coingig. These are real life equivalent of sites like Elance and Fiverr but in the Bitcoin ecosystem.

• Advertising: The advertising industry in the Bitcoin economy is, not surprisingly, pretty robust. This is because there are ton of new Bitcoin based services that keep coming up all the time and they all need a good advertising network.

CoinURL allows you to place Google AdSense styled ads on your website and other services like Bitads lets advertisers bid for banner space on your blog. There is also an-ads that allows you to make money through ad impressions without reference to the clicks (so it isn't PPC). If you're a publisher - blogger or webmaster, you can earn some Bitcoins through this route.

• Going Social: There are sites that will pay you for your activity. CoinChat is perhaps the best known site in this category. It pays users a few milli-Bitcoins for chatting on their site. These are random and controlled by an algorithm that takes into account your activity and how well you're contributing to the discussions at hand.

• Another way in which a lot of Bitcoin enthusiasts earn some Bitcoin is by selling their forum signatures at Bitcointalk forums. There are a good number of advertisers who are willing to do this, and for the socially active member who values interaction through this forum (it is the same forum through which Satoshi Nakamoto introduced Bitcoin to the world), selling signatures can be lucrative.

BEST BITCOIN SITES

Here are the best Bitcoin sites that will allow you to earn Bitcoin online. If you're looking to make some Bitcoin performing small tasks online, then this is the perfect list for you. I update this list regularly, with only the best sites out there.

The Bitcoin economy is a fast changing one, and there are several sites that come up that allow you to make some Bitcoin online. You should remember that this can also be a time-trap and you can get sucked into it for long hours without having much to show for it. This is why you need to filter these down.

A special mention to online wallets like Circle and Coinbase that make it really easy to buy and sell Bitcoin to a lay-person. Of course, if you have substantial amount of Bitcoin (over 5 BTC), get a Trezor or KeepKey – hardware wallets that stores your Bitcoin offline in a secure enclave.

1. BitcoinGet: The popular site that was mentioned in the Wired article on how homeless guys were able to use BitcoinGet as a form of 'digital hustling'. There are two popular ways to earn some Bitcoin here – Micro-tasks from CrowdFlower and watching Virool videos. The micro-tasks pay anywhere from 30-600uBTC depending on the task, and there are several tasks that you can do in a single day. The virool videos currently pay 40uBTC for 30 seconds of video. Availability depends on the location (e.g. in the US, on an average, there are 10-12 videos per day, so you can earn close to 400-500 uBTC just through the videos and then some more from the micro-tasks). Payments are automatic, and usually processed pretty promptly within a day or two. The site has also added Surveys to the list of ways to earn Bitcoin.

2. Bitter: Bitter is the best Bitcoin PTC (paid to click) out there, which gives you Bitcions to visit advertiser sites for a set amount of time. This is the newest addition to the list, and from what I have seen so far, it's a very nice user experience and very different from other Bitcoin PTC sites that you find out there, which use standardized 'bux scripts' to run their sites. Bitter is built in HTML5, and just gives a much nicer experience overall. There

are no silly recaptchas and is privacy friendly, with access via TOR without blocking. They also don't ask for your email address, which is neat. You can reach the minimum payout every day, or every couple of days. The payments are very prompt and usually processed within the hour (of late, this is usually taking 1-2 days instead). The site is probably the best way to earn your first Bitcoins online.

3. BitsForClicks (previously Coin Ad): This has remarkably become the most popular and sustained Paid-to-Click Bitcoin site. There are several reasons — Coin Ad has a very good inventory of ads and it always has a steady supply. In addition, the minimum payout is only 150uBTC that can be reached within 2-3 days depending on how many ads are available on a day. This makes it a low risk investment in terms of time for many bidders. They have done pretty well so far — it is a relatively old site, and is growing in popularity with the advertisers.

4. iFaucet: This is the best Bitcoin faucet rotator, which can give you a fairly significant amount of satoshis for faucets if you follow all the sites. It manages the entire process for you, and is a fairly

comprehensive and updated list of all the Bitcoin faucets out there. In addition, it has very good search filters, so if you hate one type of captcha, you can remove it from the list. You can also blacklist sites that you don't like. Finally, iFaucet blocks annoying popups and other undesirable page elements, so it's a smoother browsing experience.

5. Anonymous Ads: This is my favorite Bitcoin ad network and I like this more than others like CoinURL, BitMedia, Operation Fabulous, BitAds. Unlike the others mentioned which are pay-per-click, anonymous ads is a pay-per-impression system and the payment really depends on a number of factors. The stats are amazing and everything is open for you to see. I use this on my site as well and I am happy so far. If you own a website or blog, this is a very passive way to make Bitcoin. They are perhaps the longest running ad-network for the Bitcoin community, and the owner has been a very regular member of Bitcointalk forums since the very beginning.

6. Coinality: Coinality is hands down the best jobs aggregator in the Bitcoin space. If you're interested in the Bitcoin and cryptocurrency space at all, definitely keep an eye out on Coinality. It allows

special listings on its own site, but also sources jobs from across the web from Upwork and Elance to mainstream job sites like Indeed. They also have jobs of all types, from full-time developers to freelance writers. You will find small gigs, like logo design to full-time software developer positions on companies like Coinbase.

7. Predictious: Predictious is a Bitcoin prediction market, and you could earn money by suggesting new bets/statements and also predicting the right outcomes of future events. However, be on the lookout for some new decentralized prediction markets that might eat centralized prediction markets' lunch. Most notably, Augur, built on Ethereum but allows Bitcoin bets directly, is building a fully decentralized prediction marketplace that will easily undercut Predictious in terms of trust, security, and fees. Augur has raised several millions of dollars overall.

Others

8. Ads4BTC: This is a very nice Bitcoin PTC site, quite similar to Neobux in its look and feel, but with Bitcoin payments of course. They generally have a good ad inventory, which is essential for a

long-term sustainable PTC. The ads are sorted based on the time, and the payment per ad is upfront as well. The site has a lower payout available through a microwallet, or regular Bitcoin payments as well but at a higher minimum payout.

9. ABitBack: This is another popular site to make some free Bitcoin online. The most popular service here is Radio Loyalty that pays you 1 point (30uBTC) every few minutes for just listening to the radio. Supersonic Ads and Virool Videos are also popular, although Virool videos pay less than at BitcoinGet. There is also support for Litecoin (also see how to earn Litecoin).

10. Coin Chat: This is one very great way to make some Bitcoin just chatting with your fellow Bitcoin enthusiasts and learning about everything from Bitcoin to politics to programming. You can just have fun and chill in any of the chatrooms and you'll randomly get some Bitcoins. It isn't very much, and you should do this only if you enjoy getting to know other people on the internet in the Bitcoin community, but say an hour of serious discussion can yield about 1mBTC.

11. Bit Visitor: I had to include this because it is one of the oldest, still working paid-to-click ad viewing site that pays quite well. You can reach payout almost every day because the minimum is just 100uBTC. The site has had problems on and off, but overall it has a good name in the community and attracts lots of eyeballs and businesses.

12. Daily Bitcoins: This is the only faucet I'll mention just because it is that good. It pays 10uBTC every hour. If you have the time and you spend a lot of your time online, you might as well use it every hour. Note that there are also several bonus payouts, with as high as 1000uBTC payments (rare) but several 50uBTC payouts. You'll find these under Prizes tab on the top. You'll also get several vouchers for PeerBet and coupons for advertising on that site as bonus.

13. Rewards Live: Rewards Live is quickly becoming one of my favorite site for micro-payments in Bitcoin, even though I was initially skeptical of its success. They are doing pretty well and look quite sustainable. Rewards Live perhaps has the highest number of different ways to earn Bitcoin online, which is why I would classify them

in the list of best Bitcoin sites. Here is just a snapshot: Matomy, Sponsor Pay, Radium One, Super Rewards, WallAds, RevU, Payment Wall and more being added. Even the payout options are plenty – you can withdraw via Bitcoin, Litecoin and Namecoin, but if you don't want to go via the cryptocurrency route, there are scores of gift cards where you can withdraw as well (of course, I would suggest Bitcoin/Litecoin/Namecoin!) The site is adding luck-based giveaways to the various ways to earn money, which is an added bonus.

WHERE CAN YOU BUY BITCOIN LIKE THIS?

You may have a bitcoin Meetup in your area. You can check out localbitcoins.com to find people near you who are interested in buying or selling. Some are trying to start up local street exchanges across the world. These are called Buttonwoods after the first street exchange established on Wall Street in 1792 under a buttonwood tree. See if there is one, or start one, in your area.

See if you have any friends who would like to try bitcoins out. Actually, the more people who start using bitcoin, the larger and more successful it will be come. So please tell two friends!

Some people ask if it is possible to buy physical bitcoins. The answer to this is both a yes and a no. Bitcoin, by its very nature, is a digital currency and has no physical form. However, there are a couple of ways that you can practically hold a bitcoin in your hands:

Cascascius Coins: These are the brainchild of Mike Caldwell. He mints physical coins and then embeds the private keys for the bitcoins inside them. You can get the private key by peeling a hologram from the coin which will then clearly show that the coin has been tampered with. Mike has gone out of his way to ensure that he can be trusted. These are a good investment strategy as in the years to come it may be that these coins are huge collector's items.

Paper Wallets: A paper wallet just means that rather than keeping the information for your bitcoin stored in a digital wallet, you print the key information off along with a private key and keep it safe in a safe, in a drawer, or in your mattress (if you like). This is highly recommended and cost effective system for keeping your bitcoin safe. Keep in mind, though, that someone could steal them or if your house burns, they will go with the house and there will be no way to get them back.

Really, no different than cash. Also, as with Casascius Coins, they will not really be good for spending until you put them back into the computer.

• There is software to make printing your paper wallets easier. bitcoinpaperwallet.com is one of the best and includes a good tutorial about how to use them.

• The bitcoins are not actually in the wallet, they are still on the web. In fact, the outside of the wallet will have a QR code that will allow you ship coins to the wallet any time you like.

• The sealed part of the wallet will have the private key without which you cannot access the coins. Therefore, only put as many coins on the wallet as you want to be inaccessible. You will not be able to whip this thing out and take out a few coins to buy a cup of coffee. Rather, think of it as a piggy bank. To get the money, you have to smash it. It is possible to take out smaller amounts, but at this point the security of the wallet is compromised and it would be easier for someone to steal the coins. Better to have them all in or out.

• People who use paper wallets are usually security conscious, and there are a number of ways for the nefarious in the world to hack your computer. Bitcoinpaperwallet.com gives a lot of good advice about how to print your wallets securely.

Some people have also asked about buying bitcoins on eBay. Yes, it is possible, but they will be far overpriced. So, selling on eBay might seem to be a better option given the extreme markup over market value you might see. But, as with anything that is too good to be true, this is too good to be true. As I will explain in the next section, selling bitcoin this way is just way too risky.

HOW BITCOIN WORKS

Bitcoins are a decentralized form of crypto currency. Meaning, they are not regulated by a financial institution or the government. As such, unlike a traditional bank account, you do not need a long list of paperwork such as an ID in order for you to establish what's known as a bitcoin wallet. The bitcoin wallet is what you will use to access your bitcoins and to send bitcoins to other individuals.

How Does Bitcoin Work As An Anonymous Payment Processor

You can do 3 things with bitcoins, you can make a purchase, send money anonymously to someone or utilize it as an investment. More and more merchants have been accepting bitcoins as a form of payment. By utilizing bitcoins instead of cash, you are essentially making that purchase anonymously. The same thing goes for sending money, based on the fact that you do not have to submit a mountain of payment in order for you to establish a bitcoin anonymously, essentially you can send money to someone else anonymously.

How Does Bitcoin Work As An Investment

The price of a bitcoin fluctuates from time to time. Just to put things in perspective, back in the beginning of 2013, the average price of a bitcoin was approximately $400 per bitcoin, but by the end of 2013, the price for bitcoin rose to over $1000. This meant that if you had 2 bitcoins worth $800 in the beginning of 2013 and you stored it as an investment by the end of 2013 those two bitcoins would have been worth over $2000 instead of $800. Many people store bitcoins due to the fact that the value of it fluctuates.

Bitcoin Casino and Poker Sites

Due to the anonymity of bitcoin, the gambling industry has taken up bitcoin as a payment method. Both bitcoin casinos and bitcoin poker sites are coming to life and offering their players to make deposits, play with bitcoin at the tables and withdraw directly to their bitcoin wallet. This means that there's no taxes or possibilities for government control. Much like a regular Nevada casino where you don't need to register anywhere and all your transactions are anonymous.

HOW BITCOIN WILL PROMOTE LATIN AMERICAN GROWTH

There has been much ado concerning Bitcoin and how authorities and businesses in China and the United States have reacted to it, but possibly more intriguing possibilities may lie ahead for this currency and other cryptocurrencies. The Wall Street Journal ran a piece a week ago about the obvious divide that exists in Latin America. The Atlantic facing countries have more command oriented economies while the Pacific facing countries, with the exception of Ecuador and Nicaragua, have more market-oriented economies. Latin America has become a continent of focus on a global scale with stifled European growth and an Asia-Pacific region that has already been welcomed into the global economic conversation. Alternative currencies will make their mark on Latin America and it will affect both sides in a different fashion. In the end, Bitcoin and Latin American Growth will go together as they both are in spotlight at the same time and cryptocurrencies (including Bitcoin) will afford Latin American businesses and entrepreneurs the opportunity to operate on a level playing field with the rest of the globe.

Notable State Oriented Economies of Latin America

Ecuador

Bolivia

Cuba

Brazil

Argentina

Nicaragua

Venezuela

These countries have economies that are more beholden to national interests. The most extreme state run economy on this list is Cuba, which has a Communist regime that has made slight concessions to economic liberalization. Venezuela has arguably the second most extreme state run economy and is in the midst of a socioeconomic and political crisis. Argentina has had its fair share of instability and command-oriented economic events courtesy of President Cristina Fernandez de Kirchner including price controls, drama concerning possession of the Falkland Islands, inflation of 26%, police strikes, and the nationalization of YPF just to name a few measures. Brazil is always feared to resort to its old ways and currently there is still a great deal of red tape and taxation is comparatively higher than peers.

Notable Market-Oriented Economies of Latin America

   Mexico

   Colombia

   Panama

   Chile

   Peru

   Belize

Mexico's efforts to attract and grow business is not just limited to Mexico City, but Guadalajara has been emphasized as a growth destination in the digital and tech space much like the way Bogota is the established economic powerhouse city in Colombia and Medellin has broken out a youthful, digital force. Mexico is currently the 14th largest economy and growing. Mexico is still plagued by the drug cartels as demand for drugs across the northern border still exists. Ciudad Juarez is plagued by cartel-induced violence, which is considered so bad that the Sun Bowl strongly discouraged visitors from traveling across the border as the college bowl game was an opportunity to promote both El Paso, Texas and Ciudad Juarez for tourism and business.

Colombia is still combatting FARC, but it is clearly winning the battle after President Uribe's term. FARC has been more limited to the jungle areas of Colombia. Active peace talks with FARC are also being negotiated to an extent. The Colombian economy has much room to grow in terms of agriculture, energy, finance, tourism, and digital technology.

Belize is actively courting Americans to purchase real estate in the country marketing their pristine beaches, tax policies, and English fluency. Belize has a lot more growing to do and it has to shake stigmas.

Chile is considered by the Heritage Foundation to be #1 in economic freedom in Latin America. Chile enjoys a trade surplus, a central bank policy rate of 4.5% that would be attractive to investors outside of Chile. Trading the Chilean Peso may be a worthy endeavor for those wishing to take advantage of the carry trade against countries/economic zones that have extremely low interest rates such as the United States, European Union, and Japan. Chile has low inflation and has policies that benefit not just copper exports, but other exports to help maintain the surplus. Morgan Stanley expects Chile, Peru, Colombia, and Mexico to grow on average 4.25% in 2014.

These countries are not facing looting outbreaks, fights over toilet paper, nor do they have leaders that are trying to escalate action against another country.

Bitcoin's Impact on State-Oriented Economies

In all of these state-oriented economies, there are currency controls. Venezuela and Argentina are infamous for their price controls. Brazil's government influence in the economy stems from their excessive influence, possible corruption issues, and inflationary concerns. Entrepreneurs, investors, and ordinary individuals will be looking to the marketplace to meet their needs. Rationing, red tape, high costs, and possible surveillance are associated with these state-oriented economies. Bitcoin and cryptocurrencies will meet the needs of many that have access to the internet.

Competing globally in countries that wish to be more insular comes with negative ramifications, but the usage of the internet and the ability to transact in a possibly untraced fashion in a global marketplace will enable competitive pricing for citizens to receive the goods and services needed. Venezuelans will be able to buy toilet paper from foreign sources without having to use a currency that is being grossly debased. Venezuelans will also have the opportunity to engage in entrepreneurship while still in Venezuela to fund their endeavors and possible defection to other countries such as Colombia. Over 26% of Venezuelans use the internet on a daily basis. Venezuela has not filtered the internet just yet and purchasing Bitcoin is far more secure than holding onto Bolivar.

Bitcoin usage could take the government's tight grip on the economy away by rendering its presence useless by adopting the private currency. Less tax revenues can be collected, a populace that is armed financially and possibly literally (you could have bought anything on Silk Road), and decreased influence from political leaders and enforcers as cryptocurrency usage becomes viral. This thought process can be applied to Venezuela-lite in Argentina, which is an economy with a lot of potential.

The Brazilian economy could grow further by giving businesses more exposure overseas and overcoming the exotic sovereign currency issue. The World Cup in 2014 and Olympics in 2016 will put much pressure on the Brazilian economy to grow and keep up appearances. Lower transaction costs, currency familiarity, and nationality ambivalence with Bitcoin customers will help Brazilian firms seeking to do business outside of Brazil. With a large influx of tourists and business-people coming to Rio de Janeiro and São Paulo, the acceptance of Bitcoin and other cryptocurrencies will remove the barriers of having to convert currencies and engage in secure purchases. Brazil may be a more command-oriented economy like Argentina, but global expectations and aspirations should push them away from past tendencies.

For the state-oriented economies, Bitcoin and its competitors offer greater freedom, monetary security, entrepreneurship opportunities, transaction security, and privacy. In the case of Venezuela, it could spark a change in governance much like the way social media was credited for bringing in the Arab Spring to life. Much of the problems surrounding Venezuela are economic in nature and the black market is a natural alternative. Prevention of seizure of assets by keeping them in a digital wallet in the cloud is far more secure than keeping funds in a bank regulated by the Venezuelan government.

Bitcoin's Role in Economic Growth for the Pacific Countries

Entrepreneurship as described in the previous section is on a smaller level than what may be in Colombia, Mexico, Chile, and Peru. Colombia and Mexico have cities that have hopes to global players in the digital space. Attracting business from Europe, Canada, and the United States would be easier with lower exchange and transaction fees. Credit cards and PayPal place transaction fees on users wishing to make international transactions and this fee would be reduced.

Latin American outsourcing can experience growth as call centers, development and design firms, and independent contractors are able to not only competitively bid as they do now, but they would be able to accept Bitcoin and other cryptocurrencies and this will drive in more business. It is not a fad, it is a matter of making an easier and cheaper transaction. Less barriers to making the purchase will make the sale and it will help Latin American businesses to be able to be global, which can lead to Venture Capital growth.

Bitcoin will lead to greater international business transactions for Latin America and enable economic growth. The benefits are different for these countries as the need for stability is not pressing, but rather these countries have an insatiable appetite for growth. Entrepreneurship, competing globally, lower transaction fees, transactional security, competitive biddng, improved economic development, and changing perceptions are all benefits of adopting cryptocurrencies in these countries. A startup in Medellin or Cartagena can compete with a firm in Toronto and another firm in Indianapolis for a services contract. Removing the barriers of nationality from the transaction to focus solely on the services provided and costs involved are a major benefit.

Consumers win too in these countries as they would gain purchasing power because some items are more expensive in their domestic markets than foreign markets. Ex-pats and immigrants can send money to family members in their native country in a simple, inexpensive, quick, and secure fashion. This can help boost local economies.

Bitcoin and other cryptocurrencies help make the world a smaller place just like the way air travel, the internet, telecommunications, and social media have done. Cryptocurrencies promote globalization and Bitcoin will help provide that opportunity to Latin America, which is eager to compete and grow in the global marketplace.

CONCLUSION

Bitcoins are not printed like traditional currencies as there are no physical representations for the cryptocurrency; it is produced by users and numerous businesses through a process called mining. This is where dedicated software solves mathematical problems in exchange for the virtual currency.

A user takes control of it using electronic devices, which also serves as medium to complete transactions with the help of numerous platforms. It is also kept and secured with the employment of virtual wallets.

Bitcoin has the characteristics of traditional currencies such as purchasing power, and investment applications using online trading instruments. It works just like conventional money, only in the sense that it can only exist in the digital world.

One of its unique attributes that cannot be matched by fiat currency is that it is decentralized. The currency does not run under a governing body or an institution, which means it cannot be controlled by these entities, giving users full ownership of their bitcoins.

Moreover, transactions occur with the use of Bitcoin addresses, which are not linked to any names, addresses, or any personal information asked for by traditional payment systems.

Every single Bitcoin transaction is stored in a ledger anyone can access, this is called the blockchain. If a user has a publicly used address, its information is shared for everyone to see, without its user's information of course.

Accounts are easy to create, unlike conventional banks that requests for countless information, which may put its users in jeopardy due to the frauds and schemes surrounding the system.

Furthermore, Bitcoin transactions fees will always be small in number. Apart from near-instant completion of processing, no fees are known to be significant enough to put a dent on one's account

Apart from its abilities to purchase goods and services, one of its known applications features is its use for a number of investment vehicles. This includes Forex, trading Bitcoins, and binary options platforms. Furthermore, brands offer services that revolve around Bitcoin as currency.

Clearly, Bitcoin is as flexible as traditional legal tenders. Its introduction provides every individual with new beneficial opportunities with its ease of use and profit making capabilities.

Finally, if you enjoyed this book, then I'd like to ask you for a favor, would you be kind enough to leave a review for this book on Amazon? It'd be greatly appreciated!

Thank you and good luck!

I truly do appreciate it!

Best Wishes,

Lee Maxwell

www.ingramcontent.com/pod-product-compliance
Lightning Source LLC
Chambersburg PA
CBHW051723170526
45167CB00002B/771